Please visit
www.stacieoverman.com/gift
For your free gift!

Angel Kisses *Every Day*

THE JOURNAL

A Chance to Communicate and Heal with Angels Every Day

STACIE OVERMAN

FOUNDER OF THE NEW YOU PROGRAMS

To the woman warriors who have conquered
so much in this lifetime!
Knowing there is much more for them
in this incarnation,
and having the courage to go within
even when it feels scary.

Dear Beautiful Soul,

This journal contains messages given to me by Angels – my "Spirit Team" – when I was close to death, during my recovery, and up until the present day.

The Angel messages are here to lift you up and inspire you to connect with your own "Spirit Team"!

Although the entire story can be found in my book, *Angel Kisses No More Cancer (http://tiny.cc/angelkisses-nomorecancer)*, this journey has led me to a singular devotion: helping other beautiful souls like *you* find their own highest Divine Truth!

I am so glad you are here. *So are your Angels!*

Journaling consistently provides significant benefits. It allows you to: recognize patterns, heal blockages, track your progress, understand divine messages coming through to you, *and so much more*!

Learning to connect with your Angels is like learning a new language. Journaling will help you master this life-changing skill!

The following pages contain tips and inspiration for you as you build your skills. However, the single most important tip I have for you today is: breathe deeply and remember: *you are loved and cared for!*

THANK YOU FOR BEING HERE! REMEMBER: YOU ARE NOT ALONE. YOU ARE NEVER ALONE!

Love,

I f you are reading this, you've already taken the first and most crucial steps in communicating with your own Angels and "Spirit Team": believing it is possible, and setting the intention to connect.

Here are some tips & reminders of ways to connect with your Angels! *As mentioned, journaling will help you track your progress and growth.*

SUGGESTIONS

- Meditate before journaling

- Date your pages

- Each session, make note of what you feel, see, hear, smell or just know

- It's important to write down messages you receive in order to help you make sense of bigger messages

BE CONTENT IN YOUR OWN QUIET MIND

- Quieting our mind through meditation helps us to stay grounded and discern the difference between our own thoughts and any Divine messages that come to you

MEDITATION: FIND OUT WHO YOU REALLY ARE

Before journaling, quiet your mind. Practice being present. Create physical and mental calmness.

INSTRUCTIONS

- Eliminate distractions

- Relax & get comfy

- Choose your pose

- Focus your mind

- Breathe slowly and deeply

- When your mind wanders, gently say *"thank you but not now"*

- Breathe

- Gently end your meditation

Can you commit to 5 minutes a day?

Please feel free to come join and SHARE what you receive in the
Understanding Divine Messages facebook group!
http://tiny.cc/divinemessages

DATE

☐ **I MEDITATED**!

☐ I HEREBY ACCEPT AND REMEMBER THAT **I AM LOVED DEARLY**

NOTES ABOUT WHAT I FEEL, HEAR, SMELL OR KNOW:

_____

_____

_____

_____

_____

_____

_____

_____

_____

_____

_____

_____

R emember that only love is real. God and Angels have so much love for you – no matter what you are going through.

DOES THIS ANGEL MESSAGE HAVE SIGNIFICANCE TO ME?

DATE

☐ **I MEDITATED**!

☐ I HEREBY ACCEPT AND REMEMBER THAT **I AM LOVED DEARLY**

NOTES ABOUT WHAT I FEEL, HEAR, SMELL OR KNOW:

_____

_____

_____

_____

_____

_____

_____

_____

_____

_____

_____

God uses all things for good. When you are in the midst of your darkness, know that there is still light and, dear ones, we also know that sometimes it feels hopeless.

DOES THIS ANGEL MESSAGE HAVE SIGNIFICANCE TO ME?

DATE

☐ **I MEDITATED**!

☐ I HEREBY ACCEPT AND REMEMBER THAT **I AM LOVED DEARLY**

NOTES ABOUT WHAT I FEEL, HEAR, SMELL OR KNOW:

_____

_____

_____

_____

_____

_____

_____

_____

_____

_____

_____

Life can be so challenging, throwing many wrenches in the mix... Why me, you ask? Because you, dear one, have asked for this contrast. You've asked for help to focus on the God within, to help you focus on the love, to help you expand your light, to expand in this lifetime, to expand to a greater level, dear ones.

DOES THIS ANGEL MESSAGE HAVE SIGNIFICANCE TO ME?

_____

_____

_____

_____

_____

_____

_____

_____

_____

_____

DATE

☐ **I MEDITATED!**

☐ I HEREBY ACCEPT AND REMEMBER THAT **I AM LOVED DEARLY**

NOTES ABOUT WHAT I FEEL, HEAR, SMELL OR KNOW:

Y ou came here to experience things, and you have forgotten that we are here as guardians, as your "spirit team" as Stacie calls us – here to lovingly nudge you, lovingly encourage you, lovingly protect you, and help you.

DOES THIS ANGEL MESSAGE HAVE SIGNIFICANCE TO ME?

DATE

☐ **I MEDITATED!**

☐ I HEREBY ACCEPT AND REMEMBER THAT **I AM LOVED DEARLY**

NOTES ABOUT WHAT I FEEL, HEAR, SMELL OR KNOW:

Y ou must be open to loving yourself. We find that the human consciousness, the human side of people has the tendency to — how do we say, forget the necessity of loving oneself.

DOES THIS ANGEL MESSAGE HAVE SIGNIFICANCE TO ME?

DATE

☐ **I MEDITATED**!

☐ I HEREBY ACCEPT AND REMEMBER THAT **I AM LOVED DEARLY**

NOTES ABOUT WHAT I FEEL, HEAR, SMELL OR KNOW:

G od has assigned us these beautiful Angels—beautiful spirit teams—to lift us up, hold us underneath each arm, and help us to walk when we feel we cannot walk.

DOES THIS ANGEL MESSAGE HAVE SIGNIFICANCE TO ME?

DATE

☐ **I MEDITATED!**

☐ I HEREBY ACCEPT AND REMEMBER THAT **I AM LOVED DEARLY**

NOTES ABOUT WHAT I FEEL, HEAR, SMELL OR KNOW:

O ur advice to you, dear ones, is to learn how to be. How to be, how to listen, how to just be in the moment so you do not get yourself into a place of having to deal with disease in your human, physical body.

DOES THIS ANGEL MESSAGE HAVE SIGNIFICANCE TO ME?

DATE

☐ **I MEDITATED**!

☐ I HEREBY ACCEPT AND REMEMBER THAT **I AM LOVED DEARLY**

NOTES ABOUT WHAT I FEEL, HEAR, SMELL OR KNOW:

R eally coming at it from a loving heart is going to empower us for change, empower us to get through these tough times.

DOES THIS ANGEL MESSAGE HAVE SIGNIFICANCE TO ME?

DATE

☐ **I MEDITATED**!

☐ I HEREBY ACCEPT AND REMEMBER THAT **I AM LOVED DEARLY**

NOTES ABOUT WHAT I FEEL, HEAR, SMELL OR KNOW:

W**e are always here for you, we are always a breath away, we are always a prayer away.**

DOES THIS ANGEL MESSAGE HAVE SIGNIFICANCE TO ME?

_____

_____

_____

_____

_____

_____

_____

_____

_____

DATE

☐ **I MEDITATED**!

☐ I HEREBY ACCEPT AND REMEMBER THAT **I AM LOVED DEARLY**

NOTES ABOUT WHAT I FEEL, HEAR, SMELL OR KNOW:

Beloved, you have a mission and we are here to help you to align with that mission—aligning with the mission allows you to expand in your consciousness, it allows you to expand in this lifetime.

DOES THIS ANGEL MESSAGE HAVE SIGNIFICANCE TO ME?

DATE

☐ **I MEDITATED**!

☐ I HEREBY ACCEPT AND REMEMBER THAT **I AM LOVED DEARLY**

NOTES ABOUT WHAT I FEEL, HEAR, SMELL OR KNOW:

It is so easy to slip into a low-vibrational frequency when we are focused on all the lower frequencies. Just asking you to surrender the negative thinking, you have control over your thoughts, so as these negative thoughts encroach into your mind, release them.

DOES THIS ANGEL MESSAGE HAVE SIGNIFICANCE TO ME?

DATE

☐ **I MEDITATED!**

☐ I HEREBY ACCEPT AND REMEMBER THAT **I AM LOVED DEARLY**

NOTES ABOUT WHAT I FEEL, HEAR, SMELL OR KNOW:

RELISH in the gift. RECEIVE the gift, dear ones. RECEIVE the gift. You are worthy of this gift. God has this gift waiting just for you.

DOES THIS ANGEL MESSAGE HAVE SIGNIFICANCE TO ME?

_____

_____

_____

_____

_____

_____

_____

_____

_____

_____

DATE

☐ **I MEDITATED!**

☐ I HEREBY ACCEPT AND REMEMBER THAT **I AM LOVED DEARLY**

NOTES ABOUT WHAT I FEEL, HEAR, SMELL OR KNOW:

W e are sending all of you love, from our hearts to yours.

DOES THIS ANGEL MESSAGE HAVE SIGNIFICANCE TO ME?

DATE

☐ **I MEDITATED**!

☐ I HEREBY ACCEPT AND REMEMBER THAT **I AM LOVED DEARLY**

NOTES ABOUT WHAT I FEEL, HEAR, SMELL OR KNOW:

If it takes time for you to be childlike, live childlike, create time and space for you to be playful, be silly, laugh, and enjoy doing things that you are not so stressed and worried about. The particulars—every day—day in and day out—it is imperative to nurture the inner child.

DOES THIS ANGEL MESSAGE HAVE SIGNIFICANCE TO ME?

DATE

☐ **I MEDITATED!**

☐ I HEREBY ACCEPT AND REMEMBER THAT **I AM LOVED DEARLY**

NOTES ABOUT WHAT I FEEL, HEAR, SMELL OR KNOW:

I t is our job to help lovingly guide you. Your spirit team, as Stacie calls it, is never far away. We are always right there, near you, by you, with you.

DOES THIS ANGEL MESSAGE HAVE SIGNIFICANCE TO ME?

_____

_____

_____

_____

_____

_____

_____

_____

DATE

☐ **I MEDITATED!**

☐ I HEREBY ACCEPT AND REMEMBER THAT **I AM LOVED DEARLY**

NOTES ABOUT WHAT I FEEL, HEAR, SMELL OR KNOW:

Everything happens in divine order, so have faith, dear ones. We have never left you, we will never leave you, we are beside you, we are around you, we are with you. Call us any time you are wanting us to help. You must ask.

DOES THIS ANGEL MESSAGE HAVE SIGNIFICANCE TO ME?

_____

_____

_____

_____

_____

_____

_____

_____

_____

_____

DATE

☐ **I MEDITATED!**

☐ I HEREBY ACCEPT AND REMEMBER THAT **I AM LOVED DEARLY**

NOTES ABOUT WHAT I FEEL, HEAR, SMELL OR KNOW:

S ometimes you feel like giving up, surrendering, and coming home because you see or feel a lack of God/Source/light, But we assure you, dear ones, the divine is guiding you each step of the way.

DOES THIS ANGEL MESSAGE HAVE SIGNIFICANCE TO ME?

DATE

☐ **I MEDITATED**!

☐ I HEREBY ACCEPT AND REMEMBER THAT **I AM LOVED DEARLY**

NOTES ABOUT WHAT I FEEL, HEAR, SMELL OR KNOW:

We will shine light on each step as you go, dear one.

DOES THIS ANGEL MESSAGE HAVE SIGNIFICANCE TO ME?

DATE

☐ **I MEDITATED!**

☐ I HEREBY ACCEPT AND REMEMBER THAT **I AM LOVED DEARLY**

NOTES ABOUT WHAT I FEEL, HEAR, SMELL OR KNOW:

We come to you through friendships, we come to you through families, we come to you through music, we come to you through song, through numbers, through different venues, and we encourage each and every one of you to pay attention to those signs.

DOES THIS ANGEL MESSAGE HAVE SIGNIFICANCE TO ME?

_____

_____

_____

_____

_____

_____

_____

_____

_____

DATE

☐ **I MEDITATED**!

☐ I HEREBY ACCEPT AND REMEMBER THAT **I AM LOVED DEARLY**

NOTES ABOUT WHAT I FEEL, HEAR, SMELL OR KNOW:

_____

_____

_____

_____

_____

_____

_____

_____

_____

_____

_____

Allow that inner child to come out and play. Allow the time needed to heal your heart, heal the wounds that have happened, heal so that the walls may melt away and that you can expand that love and give a greater sense to the entire world.

DOES THIS ANGEL MESSAGE HAVE SIGNIFICANCE TO ME?

DATE

☐ **I MEDITATED!**

☐ I HEREBY ACCEPT AND REMEMBER THAT **I AM LOVED DEARLY**

NOTES ABOUT WHAT I FEEL, HEAR, SMELL OR KNOW:

W e want you to know that we are all connected, we are all tied together, we are all a part of this greater love.

DOES THIS ANGEL MESSAGE HAVE SIGNIFICANCE TO ME?

_____

_____

_____

_____

_____

_____

_____

_____

_____

DATE

☐ **I MEDITATED!**

☐ I HEREBY ACCEPT AND REMEMBER THAT **I AM LOVED DEARLY**

NOTES ABOUT WHAT I FEEL, HEAR, SMELL OR KNOW:

KNOW that your SELF is healed. Open your arms to receive God's gifts for you, await the reveal, untie the bow, open the lid, remove the tissue, and pull out the gift.

DOES THIS ANGEL MESSAGE HAVE SIGNIFICANCE TO ME?

_____

_____

_____

_____

_____

_____

_____

_____

DATE

☐ **I MEDITATED**!

☐ I HEREBY ACCEPT AND REMEMBER THAT **I AM LOVED DEARLY**

NOTES ABOUT WHAT I FEEL, HEAR, SMELL OR KNOW:

We ask that you pull back and look from an angelic point of view—to see from a higher perspective what you are going through even though it might feel as though it could not be any worse.

DOES THIS ANGEL MESSAGE HAVE SIGNIFICANCE TO ME?

DATE

☐ **I MEDITATED!**

☐ I HEREBY ACCEPT AND REMEMBER THAT **I AM LOVED DEARLY**

NOTES ABOUT WHAT I FEEL, HEAR, SMELL OR KNOW:

We want you to know we are all connected, we are all tied together, we are all a part of this greater love.

DOES THIS ANGEL MESSAGE HAVE SIGNIFICANCE TO ME?

_____

_____

_____

_____

_____

_____

_____

_____

DATE

☐ **I MEDITATED!**

☐ I HEREBY ACCEPT AND REMEMBER THAT **I AM LOVED DEARLY**

NOTES ABOUT WHAT I FEEL, HEAR, SMELL OR KNOW:

Beloveds, we remind you the vessel is just temporary. Your soul lives on. Your soul just transforms into a different perspective. Many of you grieve the loss of a loved one. We say to you: heal, dear ones. Allow yourself time to heal but know they have never left you. They are right there. We are there. We are right there. God is right there. We are all one.

DOES THIS ANGEL MESSAGE HAVE SIGNIFICANCE TO ME?

DATE

☐ **I MEDITATED**!

☐ I HEREBY ACCEPT AND REMEMBER THAT **I AM LOVED DEARLY**

NOTES ABOUT WHAT I FEEL, HEAR, SMELL OR KNOW:

_____

_____

_____

_____

_____

_____

_____

_____

_____

_____

_____

Trust the understanding that is within you. Understand that there are messages—do not distrust those messages.

DOES THIS ANGEL MESSAGE HAVE SIGNIFICANCE TO ME?

DATE

☐ **I MEDITATED**!

☐ I HEREBY ACCEPT AND REMEMBER THAT **I AM LOVED DEARLY**

NOTES ABOUT WHAT I FEEL, HEAR, SMELL OR KNOW:

We need to stand in our power and receive these blessings... receive... reminding us to give away the fear.

DOES THIS ANGEL MESSAGE HAVE SIGNIFICANCE TO ME?

_____

_____

_____

_____

_____

_____

_____

_____

_____

DATE

☐ **I MEDITATED**!

☐ I HEREBY ACCEPT AND REMEMBER THAT **I AM LOVED DEARLY**

NOTES ABOUT WHAT I FEEL, HEAR, SMELL OR KNOW:

We want to remind you that you, too, are going through your journey and you can call upon us, and we will help to guide you back on to the road that is the easier road. This, too, shall pass.

DOES THIS ANGEL MESSAGE HAVE SIGNIFICANCE TO ME?

DATE

☐ **I MEDITATED**!

☐ I HEREBY ACCEPT AND REMEMBER THAT **I AM LOVED DEARLY**

NOTES ABOUT WHAT I FEEL, HEAR, SMELL OR KNOW:

_____

_____

_____

_____

_____

_____

_____

_____

_____

_____

_____

We as a collective want you to know that we are here for you, dear ones. We are here . . . We are here . . . You just need to call upon us—call out in prayer, call out asking, knowing that we will be there.

DOES THIS ANGEL MESSAGE HAVE SIGNIFICANCE TO ME?

DATE

☐ **I MEDITATED**!

☐ I HEREBY ACCEPT AND REMEMBER THAT **I AM LOVED DEARLY**

NOTES ABOUT WHAT I FEEL, HEAR, SMELL OR KNOW:

Y ou must love yourself, you must act out self-love. If you are giving love you must receive love.

DOES THIS ANGEL MESSAGE HAVE SIGNIFICANCE TO ME?

DATE

☐ **I MEDITATED**!

☐ I HEREBY ACCEPT AND REMEMBER THAT **I AM LOVED DEARLY**

NOTES ABOUT WHAT I FEEL, HEAR, SMELL OR KNOW:

A loving heart encourages us to really use the power we have within us, setting the intention to be able to manifest a healthy body, to be able to manifest all the blessings that we deserve in this life. Be really able to muster up all the strength within us and take back our power so we can have the authority to manifest healing—as God wants us to have this healing.

DOES THIS ANGEL MESSAGE HAVE SIGNIFICANCE TO ME?

DATE

☐ **I MEDITATED**!

☐ I HEREBY ACCEPT AND REMEMBER THAT **I AM LOVED DEARLY**

NOTES ABOUT WHAT I FEEL, HEAR, SMELL OR KNOW:

You can call on Archangel Raphael to bring about healing in a quicker way to manifest that in a quicker, more positive style.

DOES THIS ANGEL MESSAGE HAVE SIGNIFICANCE TO ME?

DATE

☐ **I MEDITATED**!

☐ I HEREBY ACCEPT AND REMEMBER THAT **I AM LOVED DEARLY**

NOTES ABOUT WHAT I FEEL, HEAR, SMELL OR KNOW:

_____

_____

_____

_____

_____

_____

_____

_____

_____

_____

_____

_____

Be allowing, be open, be receptive to receiving, have the belief that you will be healed, have the belief that you are worthy of being healed, dear ones.

DOES THIS ANGEL MESSAGE HAVE SIGNIFICANCE TO ME?

DATE

☐ **I MEDITATED!**

☐ I HEREBY ACCEPT AND REMEMBER THAT **I AM LOVED DEARLY**

NOTES ABOUT WHAT I FEEL, HEAR, SMELL OR KNOW:

D o not withhold from the love that is coming to you. Allow yourself to open and receive these gifts, dear ones. Open your arms and receive.

DOES THIS ANGEL MESSAGE HAVE SIGNIFICANCE TO ME?

_____

_____

_____

_____

_____

_____

_____

_____

_____

DATE

☐ **I MEDITATED**!

☐ I HEREBY ACCEPT AND REMEMBER THAT **I AM LOVED DEARLY**

NOTES ABOUT WHAT I FEEL, HEAR, SMELL OR KNOW:

We encourage you to know you have never been alone, you are always . . . always in the presence of God and our team of angels.

DOES THIS ANGEL MESSAGE HAVE SIGNIFICANCE TO ME?

DATE

☐ **I MEDITATED**!

☐ I HEREBY ACCEPT AND REMEMBER THAT **I AM LOVED DEARLY**

NOTES ABOUT WHAT I FEEL, HEAR, SMELL OR KNOW:

S et your intentions and manifest great health and manifest great healing and RECEIVE the gift.

DOES THIS ANGEL MESSAGE HAVE SIGNIFICANCE TO ME?

DATE

☐ **I MEDITATED!**

☐ I HEREBY ACCEPT AND REMEMBER THAT **I AM LOVED DEARLY**

NOTES ABOUT WHAT I FEEL, HEAR, SMELL OR KNOW:

We are here to help you stay aligned with your mission.

DOES THIS ANGEL MESSAGE HAVE SIGNIFICANCE TO ME?

DATE

☐ **I MEDITATED**!

☐ I HEREBY ACCEPT AND REMEMBER THAT **I AM LOVED DEARLY**

NOTES ABOUT WHAT I FEEL, HEAR, SMELL OR KNOW:

A nd we say that miracles do happen; miracles happen every day, countless times a day, every second, every minute, every hour, miracles are happening. Believe and you shall receive, dear ones.

DOES THIS ANGEL MESSAGE HAVE SIGNIFICANCE TO ME?

_____

_____

_____

_____

_____

_____

_____

_____

DATE

☐ **I MEDITATED**!

☐ I HEREBY ACCEPT AND REMEMBER THAT **I AM LOVED DEARLY**

NOTES ABOUT WHAT I FEEL, HEAR, SMELL OR KNOW:

R emember to be playful, to be silly, and to be childlike

DOES THIS ANGEL MESSAGE HAVE SIGNIFICANCE TO ME?

DATE

☐ **I MEDITATED!**

☐ I HEREBY ACCEPT AND REMEMBER THAT **I AM LOVED DEARLY**

NOTES ABOUT WHAT I FEEL, HEAR, SMELL OR KNOW:

W e are here, constantly sending you messages—divine messages.

DOES THIS ANGEL MESSAGE HAVE SIGNIFICANCE TO ME?

DATE

☐ **I MEDITATED!**

☐ I HEREBY ACCEPT AND REMEMBER THAT **I AM LOVED DEARLY**

NOTES ABOUT WHAT I FEEL, HEAR, SMELL OR KNOW:

Y ou are beloved, you are loved, we are all connected, so being in a state of love-consciousness, we encourage you to go within, to look within, and to remember that it is imperative that you love yourself.

DOES THIS ANGEL MESSAGE HAVE SIGNIFICANCE TO ME?

_____

_____

_____

_____

_____

_____

_____

_____

DATE

☐ **I MEDITATED**!

☐ I HEREBY ACCEPT AND REMEMBER THAT **I AM LOVED DEARLY**

NOTES ABOUT WHAT I FEEL, HEAR, SMELL OR KNOW:

And we say that miracles do happen; miracles happen every day, countless times a day, every second, every minute, every hour, miracles are happening. Believe and you shall receive, dear ones.

DOES THIS ANGEL MESSAGE HAVE SIGNIFICANCE TO ME?

DATE

☐ **I MEDITATED**!

☐ I HEREBY ACCEPT AND REMEMBER THAT **I AM LOVED DEARLY**

NOTES ABOUT WHAT I FEEL, HEAR, SMELL OR KNOW:

W e encourage you to stay positive. Positive affirmations are very much encouraged to keep your spirits high.

DOES THIS ANGEL MESSAGE HAVE SIGNIFICANCE TO ME?

DATE

☐ **I MEDITATED!**

☐ I HEREBY ACCEPT AND REMEMBER THAT **I AM LOVED DEARLY**

NOTES ABOUT WHAT I FEEL, HEAR, SMELL OR KNOW:

S hare your story and come into the fullness—the beauty of the contrast which is God's light.

DOES THIS ANGEL MESSAGE HAVE SIGNIFICANCE TO ME?

DATE

☐ **I MEDITATED!**

☐ I HEREBY ACCEPT AND REMEMBER THAT **I AM LOVED DEARLY**

NOTES ABOUT WHAT I FEEL, HEAR, SMELL OR KNOW:

A soul never dies. Even though we experience life and death (as you know it) alongside you, we experience the heartbreak, we experience the feeling of loss with you side by side.

DOES THIS ANGEL MESSAGE HAVE SIGNIFICANCE TO ME?

_____

_____

_____

_____

_____

_____

_____

_____

DATE

☐ **I MEDITATED**!

☐ I HEREBY ACCEPT AND REMEMBER THAT **I AM LOVED DEARLY**

NOTES ABOUT WHAT I FEEL, HEAR, SMELL OR KNOW:

We encourage you to be true to yourself. We encourage you to stand in the present moment and be you.

DOES THIS ANGEL MESSAGE HAVE SIGNIFICANCE TO ME?

DATE

☐ **I MEDITATED**!

☐ I HEREBY ACCEPT AND REMEMBER THAT **I AM LOVED DEARLY**

NOTES ABOUT WHAT I FEEL, HEAR, SMELL OR KNOW:

F eel the love in your heart. Allow yourself to heal. Allow yourself to feel the emotions and begin to remember who you are: a beautiful, divine being.

DOES THIS ANGEL MESSAGE HAVE SIGNIFICANCE TO ME?

DATE

☐ **I MEDITATED**!

☐ I HEREBY ACCEPT AND REMEMBER THAT **I AM LOVED DEARLY**

NOTES ABOUT WHAT I FEEL, HEAR, SMELL OR KNOW:

Dear one, dear one, we encourage you to take the time to nurture that inner child in you.

DOES THIS ANGEL MESSAGE HAVE SIGNIFICANCE TO ME?

DATE

☐ **I MEDITATED!**

☐ I HEREBY ACCEPT AND REMEMBER THAT **I AM LOVED DEARLY**

NOTES ABOUT WHAT I FEEL, HEAR, SMELL OR KNOW:

Many times, when we experience a thinning of the veil there will be an increased awareness that will shift your relationships, will shift your goals in life, will shift and redirect—as Stacie puts it—on to your soul's mission.

DOES THIS ANGEL MESSAGE HAVE SIGNIFICANCE TO ME?

DATE

☐ **I MEDITATED!**

☐ I HEREBY ACCEPT AND REMEMBER THAT **I AM LOVED DEARLY**

NOTES ABOUT WHAT I FEEL, HEAR, SMELL OR KNOW:

A s your angels, as your guides, we come to you in many forms. We want you to listen, to follow, to trust your intuition.

DOES THIS ANGEL MESSAGE HAVE SIGNIFICANCE TO ME?

DATE

☐ **I MEDITATED**!

☐ I HEREBY ACCEPT AND REMEMBER THAT **I AM LOVED DEARLY**

NOTES ABOUT WHAT I FEEL, HEAR, SMELL OR KNOW:

Be aware that what you bring into your reality will be your experience in this play. Everything is happening in divine order.

DOES THIS ANGEL MESSAGE HAVE SIGNIFICANCE TO ME?

DATE

☐ **I MEDITATED!**

☐ I HEREBY ACCEPT AND REMEMBER THAT **I AM LOVED DEARLY**

NOTES ABOUT WHAT I FEEL, HEAR, SMELL OR KNOW:

_____

_____

_____

_____

_____

_____

_____

_____

_____

_____

_____

_____

_____

W e ask you to look at it from a new perspective: look past the intensities that you are experiencing so you can see . . . a bigger picture.

DOES THIS ANGEL MESSAGE HAVE SIGNIFICANCE TO ME?

DATE

☐ **I MEDITATED!**

☐ I HEREBY ACCEPT AND REMEMBER THAT **I AM LOVED DEARLY**

NOTES ABOUT WHAT I FEEL, HEAR, SMELL OR KNOW:

B eloved ones, we are here with you. We are encouraging you to watch the positive mind . . . Watch the negative mind . .

DOES THIS ANGEL MESSAGE HAVE SIGNIFICANCE TO ME?

DATE

☐ **I MEDITATED!**

☐ I HEREBY ACCEPT AND REMEMBER THAT **I AM LOVED DEARLY**

NOTES ABOUT WHAT I FEEL, HEAR, SMELL OR KNOW:

It is imperative that you learn to trust and you learn to allow these divine messages to come through you. There is a reason that you are receiving these messages. If you are not trusting the messages that come, you could miss that exit, that you will miss that road. It could be a much tougher road.

DOES THIS ANGEL MESSAGE HAVE SIGNIFICANCE TO ME?

DATE

☐ **I MEDITATED**!

☐ I HEREBY ACCEPT AND REMEMBER THAT **I AM LOVED DEARLY**

NOTES ABOUT WHAT I FEEL, HEAR, SMELL OR KNOW:

There have been many signs and many more will be given whenever anyone is going through trials in this human incarnation.

DOES THIS ANGEL MESSAGE HAVE SIGNIFICANCE TO ME?

DATE

☐ **I MEDITATED!**

☐ I HEREBY ACCEPT AND REMEMBER THAT **I AM LOVED DEARLY**

NOTES ABOUT WHAT I FEEL, HEAR, SMELL OR KNOW:

We will, dear ones, use this experience to help you to realign with your soul's mission. This is very important that you start to remember, and that you see the signs. Pay attention to the signs.

DOES THIS ANGEL MESSAGE HAVE SIGNIFICANCE TO ME?

_____

_____

_____

_____

_____

_____

_____

_____

_____

DATE

☐ **I MEDITATED**!

☐ I HEREBY ACCEPT AND REMEMBER THAT **I AM LOVED DEARLY**

NOTES ABOUT WHAT I FEEL, HEAR, SMELL OR KNOW:

C oming at it from a loving heart helps us to heal on an emotional level so we can bring miracles into play. Deep... deep emotional healing is what the angels are asking us to focus on so we can get through to the next level.

DOES THIS ANGEL MESSAGE HAVE SIGNIFICANCE TO ME?

DATE

☐ **I MEDITATED**!

☐ I HEREBY ACCEPT AND REMEMBER THAT **I AM LOVED DEARLY**

NOTES ABOUT WHAT I FEEL, HEAR, SMELL OR KNOW:

C hoose to give gratitude to all.

DOES THIS ANGEL MESSAGE HAVE SIGNIFICANCE TO ME?

DATE

☐ **I MEDITATED**!

☐ I HEREBY ACCEPT AND REMEMBER THAT **I AM LOVED DEARLY**

NOTES ABOUT WHAT I FEEL, HEAR, SMELL OR KNOW:

When you can be in a place of being, in the stillness, you will receive, you will hear, you will know, and you will be guided in a much easier way to getting on track with your soul's mission.

DOES THIS ANGEL MESSAGE HAVE SIGNIFICANCE TO ME?

DATE

☐ **I MEDITATED**!

☐ I HEREBY ACCEPT AND REMEMBER THAT **I AM LOVED DEARLY**

NOTES ABOUT WHAT I FEEL, HEAR, SMELL OR KNOW:

_____

_____

_____

_____

_____

_____

_____

_____

_____

_____

_____

_____

_____

The frequency of love can heal your own vessel, your own body, your own vehicle, if you will. The frequency of love will also manifest beauty, more peace, more love, more joy to enter into your life.

DOES THIS ANGEL MESSAGE HAVE SIGNIFICANCE TO ME?

DATE

☐ **I MEDITATED!**

☐ I HEREBY ACCEPT AND REMEMBER THAT **I AM LOVED DEARLY**

NOTES ABOUT WHAT I FEEL, HEAR, SMELL OR KNOW:

W e encourage you to focus not on the loss but on the presence of your loved ones near you, around you, with you. For the soul is eternal, beloveds. The soul never dies.

DOES THIS ANGEL MESSAGE HAVE SIGNIFICANCE TO ME?

DATE

☐ **I MEDITATED**!

☐ I HEREBY ACCEPT AND REMEMBER THAT **I AM LOVED DEARLY**

NOTES ABOUT WHAT I FEEL, HEAR, SMELL OR KNOW:

Many times in life, as a human experiencing the human vessel on Earth, there comes a time when you simply need to surrender to being still. Not acting out. Just breathe. Focus on your own power within.

DOES THIS ANGEL MESSAGE HAVE SIGNIFICANCE TO ME?

DATE

☐ **I MEDITATED**!

☐ I HEREBY ACCEPT AND REMEMBER THAT **I AM LOVED DEARLY**

NOTES ABOUT WHAT I FEEL, HEAR, SMELL OR KNOW:

We encourage you, beloveds, to trust, to allow, and to go within and have self-love. To begin that healing—that sacred journey of healing—so that you may expand, so that you may experience that which you, dear ones, wanted to experience in this lifetime.

DOES THIS ANGEL MESSAGE HAVE SIGNIFICANCE TO ME?

DATE

☐ **I MEDITATED**!

☐ I HEREBY ACCEPT AND REMEMBER THAT **I AM LOVED DEARLY**

NOTES ABOUT WHAT I FEEL, HEAR, SMELL OR KNOW:

We ask you also to look for the light not only within these earth angels, but to look for the light within you. For you, dear one, are a beacon . . . a beacon of light . . . God's light . . . the light within you sparks the light in others.

DOES THIS ANGEL MESSAGE HAVE SIGNIFICANCE TO ME?

DATE

☐ **I MEDITATED**!

☐ I HEREBY ACCEPT AND REMEMBER THAT **I AM LOVED DEARLY**

NOTES ABOUT WHAT I FEEL, HEAR, SMELL OR KNOW:

C hoose life, dear ones. You chose life. You chose to come here. You chose to make a difference.

DOES THIS ANGEL MESSAGE HAVE SIGNIFICANCE TO ME?

DATE

☐ **I MEDITATED!**

☐ I HEREBY ACCEPT AND REMEMBER THAT **I AM LOVED DEARLY**

NOTES ABOUT WHAT I FEEL, HEAR, SMELL OR KNOW:

Even in the midst of these tough crises, we've never left you, and we encourage you, dear ones, to look around . . . to pay attention . . . to see the signs . . . to see the angels—the Earth Angels who have been placed in your life.

DOES THIS ANGEL MESSAGE HAVE SIGNIFICANCE TO ME?

DATE

☐ **I MEDITATED**!

☐ I HEREBY ACCEPT AND REMEMBER THAT **I AM LOVED DEARLY**

NOTES ABOUT WHAT I FEEL, HEAR, SMELL OR KNOW:

We encourage you, dear ones, to go within and love yourself, to put yourself first, to take care of this human body, to listen to the signs you are receiving, pay attention to the thoughts, pay attention to any ideas that may come to you, because, beloveds, these are answered prayers.

DOES THIS ANGEL MESSAGE HAVE SIGNIFICANCE TO ME?

DATE

☐ **I MEDITATED!**

☐ I HEREBY ACCEPT AND REMEMBER THAT **I AM LOVED DEARLY**

NOTES ABOUT WHAT I FEEL, HEAR, SMELL OR KNOW:

W e encourage you to focus not on the loss but on the presence of your loved ones near you, around you, with you. For the soul is eternal, beloveds. The soul never dies.

DOES THIS ANGEL MESSAGE HAVE SIGNIFICANCE TO ME?

DATE

☐ **I MEDITATED!**

☐ I HEREBY ACCEPT AND REMEMBER THAT **I AM LOVED DEARLY**

NOTES ABOUT WHAT I FEEL, HEAR, SMELL OR KNOW:

A ligning with your message allows you to anchor the light and to help the entire consciousness of the planet.

DOES THIS ANGEL MESSAGE HAVE SIGNIFICANCE TO ME?

Angel Kisses No More Cancer by Stacie Overman

 Stacie Overman's *Angel Kisses No More Cancer* twines the joys in the sorrows of life with cancer. From days at the chemo center to proposals at home plate, Overman is unflinchingly honest, unquestionably faithful, and unbelievably inspirational as she takes readers by the hand and introduces them to the unexplained interventions of a God who's with us in the good times and the bad."

– Bob Welch, Author

Angel Kisses No More Cancer can be ordered at: http://tiny.cc/angelkissesnomorecancer

Stacie Overman is a national speaker, spiritual coach, and author who has been guiding clients on a journey of spiritual awakening for over four years.

After surviving cancer in 2006, she found herself connecting directly and beautifully with angels, which led her to write *Angel Kisses No More Cancer*.

Founder of The New You coaching programs, Stacie's powerful supernatural gifts have been praised as "nothing short of a miracle" (Henry Jones, Massage Therapy Instructor, Texas Health School).

With a background in entrepreneurship and talent scouting, Stacie was the first spokesmodel for the Willamette Valley Cancer Institute, where she underwent her cancer treatments in Eugene, Oregon. She made an appearance in the hit series, Ghost Mine (SYFY Network).

Stacie enjoys painting angels, traveling by RV with her husband, Larry (vowing to visit every US state before they retire), and spending as much time as possible with her precious family.

Connect with Stacie at **stacieoverman.com**, as well as in her lively Facebook community
Understanding Divine Messages (*http://tiny.cc/divinemessages*)
where she helps over 7,800 lightworkers connect with spirit, heal, and enlighten the world.

PLEASE TAKE A MINUTE TO REVIEW this journal!
http://tiny.cc/angelkissesjournal

Made in the USA
Coppell, TX
16 December 2019

13065813R00083